A Step-B
Building Wealth with $1
The Black Wealth Masterclass

John D. Saunders

Paperback ISBN: 9781099775062

Cover Design: AB Baldonado

DEDICATION

For the most important people in my life, Logan, Deandra, Dawn and Alexandria, who taught me humility, compassion and love beyond measure.

I owe you EVERYTHING.

CONTENTS

The Introduction

There's a long, outdoor corridor that leads to the fitness center at Florida Atlantic University. Countless students can be seen hurriedly scurrying to class, their footsteps echoing down the long hallway.

Holding my phone clenched to my ear in fear, my voice cracks over the speaker: "But how could this happen? I've never even used my 'credit'," I said to an operator on the other line.

"Sometimes, these things happen, sir. Unfortunately, there's nothing we can do," the operator responded.

A family member had written bad checks on my name for years. As a result, my credit was shot to hell, I'd run out of scholarship funds and I needed a stipend to finish out the quarter to cover book fees, room and board and my sanity.

Not only was I TERRIBLE with money, I couldn't even get a credit card to cover a few expenses because I spent the money as soon as I got it.

In that moment, I thought back to the Pythagorean Theorem. Instead of learning the fundamentals of money management, tangible tactics I could put to work to help create wealth, I was taught that the square of a hypotenuse is equal to the sum of the squares of the other two sides. In other words, a formula that takes approximately .54 seconds to input in a Google search that I'd never use in the real world (unless I was a mathematician—which I am not).

That's the BIGGEST reason that led me to write this book. It's a culmination of principles, tips, tricks and actionable tactics you can take at any point in your life to create wealth and empower yourself with the tools to break an endless cycle. Using the principles in this book, I've been able to look intrinsically at our difficult history and leverage financial literacy to create a life that includes a multi-six figure business, healthy savings and retirement accounts and an optimistic outlook on the future.

At every point in your life, we discuss the action items you need to put in place to live a fruitful and full life—a life full of abundance, great memories, adventures and CASH FLOW.

In order to make a difference, we need to know early on that money is power and power is the influence to make CHANGE.

Welcome to the Black Wealth Masterclass.

Chapter 1 - Money and the Black Community

"Hold fast to dreams, for if dreams die, life is a broken winged bird that cannot fly." – Langston Hughes

It isn't uncommon for society to believe that racism and slavery are a distant memory, an event tucked away in the confines of American history. However, the fact is the Black community bears the brunt of long-lasting effects that slavery and racism have had on broader economic growth.

How's this for perspective? Black families in the U.S. earn just $57.30 for every $100 in income earned by White families, according to the Census Bureau's Current Population Survey.[1]

In this chapter, I'll outline the reasons behind this. In the upcoming chapters, I'll also define real tactics anyone can use at ANY age to find success in accumulating wealth.

First, let's talk about the CONCEPT of wealth.

The Concept of Wealth

By definition, wealth is the measure of a family or individual's financial net worth.

It acts as the catalyst for generational wealth, providing monetary opportunities for families in America.

Wealth makes it less of a challenge for individuals to transition, in a seamless manner, from one job to another, respond in emergency situations or move into new neighborhoods that offer growth and opportunity.

Wealth is what Americans use to partially or entirely pay for their children's education, and it helps build a solid economic foundation for retirement too.

Just imagine the opportunity afforded a young high school student who graduates with good grades, receives a college fund from his parents and begins his education at a reputable state school. As a result of the wealth accumulated by his parents, he can leverage his educational opportunity to make connections, receive a degree and begin his workforce or entrepreneurial ventures with a head start.

Aside from the items above, it's also the overall measure of the future economic well-being of a family.

The U.S. is at the top of this wealth pyramid, according to the Federal Reserve's Survey of Consumer Finances, with the average US household net worth at $692,100! Plus, that's based on data from 2016, when the S&P 500 was ~30% lower.[2]

Now, keep in mind that's the OVERALL average.

The Imbalance of Wealth in the United States

The unfortunate part of this situation is that there is an unequal distribution of wealth in America based on race.

This is especially evident between American Black and White households. African American families only possess a fraction of the wealth shared between White families. Here's the breakdown:

> According to 2016 Federal Reserve data, Blacks own about one-tenth of the wealth of White Americans. To go back to 2016, the median wealth for non-retired Black households aged 25 years and older was less than one-tenth of similarly situated White households.[3]

This puts people of color at a disadvantage as opportunities for economic mobility are hindered by an obvious gap in wealth distribution.

As a result, this discrepancy leaves people of color in a position of economic insecurity. Even with increased education levels and similar positive factors we'll discuss later in this book, Black Americans have far less wealth than White Americans in the US.

Lower income levels, compounded by lesser wealth, results in fewer education and job opportunities for people of color; in turn, this translates into dismal opportunities for upward mobility, but that isn't all.

This entire scenario has a snowball effect and Black Americans end up having fewer chances to build wealth or pass any accumulated wealth down to future generations.

The buck has to stop TODAY. At this point, you're probably asking yourself how this imbalance continues to increase over time.

What Has Created This Imbalance In Wealth?

There are a number of different factors that aggravate this vicious cycle of inequality, which leads to the startling imbalance in wealth distribution in America. Let's take a look at what some of these factors include:

Employment Discrimination

Many Black households can't easily access various tax-advantaged savings vehicles, and to a certain degree, this is due to various discriminatory practices and a lengthy history of employment discrimination.

Prior to the Federal Civil Rights Act of 1964, institutionalized discrimination denied people of color access to countless job opportunities and enforced our position at the bottom of the job queue.[4] Many of these hiring patterns and educational inequalities continued even after the Equal Pay Act of 1963 and because of the lax federal enforcement of the new civil rights laws, even high-level educational achievements of people of color couldn't dismantle history.

Mortgage Market Discrimination

This leads into why people of color become victims of mortgage market discrimination. Let's look at one scenario:

In February of last year, Wells Fargo was sued by the city of Sacramento for allegedly discriminating against Black and Latino borrowers since 2004.[5] The charge raised against the banking giant detailed how people of color were given more expensive loans than White borrowers.

Since there is comprehensive historical documentation on mortgage market discrimination, it means that people of color are far less likely to own a home as compared to White Americans.

To add a real-life example, I went through a similar predicament when purchasing my first vehicle. Basically, I found out that the bank that processed the loan was charging people of color higher interest rates for automotive loans. As a joint investigation by the U.S. Department of Justice and the Consumer Financial Protection Bureau, the bank had to pay an $18 million dollar settlement.

The bank allowed dealers to raise interest rates as they saw fit with some dealers charging customers as much as 2.5% more than the bank's actual rate, regardless of credit worthiness.

I ended up getting a $500 check.

How's that for a bit of justice?

With home ownership being one of the BEST ways to create generational wealth, people of color are already placed at a disadvantage lacking the access to tax benefits and savings that go hand in hand with owning a home.

It's a crippling trickle effect.

All of these are the key drivers by which families in the U.S are able to save money, create wealth and pass on assets to cash reserves for incoming generations.

Tax Cuts for the Rich

The last aspect that comes into view is the current tax code.

Tax code is an INSANELY long federal document detailing the rules and regulations individuals and businesses MUST follow in remitting a percentage of their incomes to the federal or state government.

Under this, families that have higher incomes are eligible for higher tax incentives related to both housing as well as retirement savings.

Unfortunately, the majority of people of color in the U.S. typically have lower income levels. This results in fewer tax benefits, especially with the lack of home ownership and lack of retirement savings accounts and home equity.

The Bottom Line

Consistent segregation, unfair labor markets and housing discrimination add fuel to the fire and worsen the cycle of wealth inequality, proving to be highly damaging to Black Americans. The Institute of Policy

Studies states that it will take Black Americans at least 228 years to cover this racial wealth gap.[6]

Through the decades, for people of color in the United States, it has been a huge task to establish a foothold in creating generational wealth. In spite of our momentous efforts and persistence, we constantly find ourselves at a disadvantage and several paces behind. Our goal is to turn this around.

ASAP.

No Ambiguity in the Data

Even when Black Americans continue with higher education, securing good jobs and purchasing homes, we're still many steps behind our White counterparts when it comes to wealth accumulation.

It's also important to note that these disparities between Black and White Americans are almost always entrenched in policies that discriminate against people of color, either explicitly or implicitly.

Statistics That Matter

There needs to be a complete shift in how we approach generational wealth as there are some significant differences in the manner in which each group handles money. Here are some stats that matter:

- When it comes to Black Americans, the wealthiest 5% of us are a little less likely to hold various financial assets like bonds stocks, etc. in our investment portfolio.
- Of the different financial assets invested in, even wealthy Blacks are far more likely (compared to well-heeled White Americans) to channel funds towards safer assets. Affluent Black Americans prefer investing in savings bonds, life insurance and CDs and will steer clear of high-reward, high-risk assets.
- Black Americans with deeper pockets invest larger amounts in real estate holdings than White Americans who are equally wealthy. The latter hold only approximately 22% of their overall non-financial assets (non-primary residence) in real estate, but with Black Americans this figure is 41%. Adding primary residences to these figures brings the numbers to 34% and 57%, respectively. Real estate continues to be looked upon as a lower-risk investment, even after the housing collapse.
- Rich Black folks are less likely to hold equity in large business assets, too. If you look at the non-financial assets of this stratum of society, only 9% is equity in business assets. For

comparably wealthy White folks, that figure stands at 37%.

- There is a stark difference in figures even when this is looked at as a percentage of total assets. Only 6% of wealthy Blacks invest in their own businesses while that figure stands at 21% in the case of wealthy White people.

- Because 23% of both these groups are equally capable of running their own businesses, researchers say it indicates that White business owners in the U.S are investing in their own businesses at an almost seven times higher rate than Black American business owners.

Steps to Take

All of these stats indicate that if the economic opportunity is to shift and generational wealth created in America, scaling Black business development and investing in Black businesses is the smartest route to take.

Currently, Black businesses supply a little over 3.56 million jobs.

This equates to approximately a fifth of the total employed Black American workforce in the country.

However, this number could easily increase if there were effective platforms in place.

These would help Black businesses of different shapes and sizes to increase revenue so that they could gradually hire more people and grow. If Black-owned businesses are able to reach employment parity with various other businesses, this could create an influx of new jobs to help reduce the rate of unemployment within the Black community.

Currently, the huge wealth chasm leaves Black entrepreneurs with significantly fewer assets and lesser income, which doesn't help us grow our businesses.

Businesses also suffer from a massive credit gap, which makes it an uphill task for people of color to easily access capital.

There has been a steady decline in the economic foundation within America's Black community that needs to be addressed and fixed via financial literacy and entrepreneurial upstarts.

But it doesn't mean corporate and individual initiatives to help us need to take the same path.

In fact, it has now become even more important than ever to find ways of investing money, energy and time into bolstering wealth within the Black community. The goal of the upcoming chapters is to provide a breakdown of the EXACT tactics to implement to create generational wealth.

Chapter 2 - The Concepts of Building Wealth

"Hold on to your dreams of a better life and stay committed to striving to realize it." – Earl G. Graves, Sr.

Whether we like it or not, money and life are closely intertwined.

When we're young, we rarely think about retirement, as most of our time is consumed with finding our way in life, whether that's through traditional education, hitting the job force full throttle or studying a trade.

However, time is precious and it's something that we never get back once it's been spent.

It also means you need to make the most of it today—whether you are pursuing your dreams, building memories with family, forging friendships or working towards your long-term career goals. This aspect is truer in the case of savings and creating a solid retirement plan.

You have to create wealth to thrive.

Create a Savings Plan for Life

The creation and proper management of wealth can be a complex task that involves various responsibilities and actions that tend to overwhelm day-to-day life.

You need to have a good understanding of and be able to integrate investment, tax and legal advice in a plan that will address your current needs in a cohesive manner. It should also allow you to slowly but surely build your savings and retirement funds. When you do this consistently, it helps you build wealth.

And WEALTH is possible for all.

According to a 2016 article from Bloomberg, 1,700 millionaires are minted every day[7]

So, it's possible for anyone of us to create substantial financial wealth, but more often than not, simply identifying the appropriate things to do can seem like an insurmountable first step. Most of us believe that establishing clear-cut goals will help us achieve success. However, it takes much more than that to create a solid and tangible savings plan that will see us through to retirement.

You Need to Have a Long-Term Vision

The very first step is to establish a more long-term vision for you as well as your family. Once you have done this, you need to approach the various aspects of your wealth as an integrated whole. Collating information, organizing all your records and keeping regular track of the process can be a little overwhelming at first.

Once you get into the groove of it and break it into monthly tasks, which are more manageable, it will help you take charge of all your financial affairs in an easier, more systematic way. If you have a good hold of the process and are consistent in your approach, it will help you manage your strategic plan for wealth-building in an appropriate manner over the years.

Going back to what I said at the outset, time is of the essence and you need to make the most of what you have NOW. Just as you focus on various other things in your life, it is equally important to make sure that you focus on building your financial stability and creating wealth.

The Cornerstones of Wealth Building

"The time is always right to do what is right."
– Dr. Martin Luther King, Jr.

Building wealth is about having three essential factors:
1. money (you don't need to start with A LOT)
2. time
3. the benefit of compound interest

It might seem like money is the most important aspect, but in relation to everything else, it's only a small piece.

In an investment formula, the most critical element is time.

The more time you have the more your compound interest will grow.

This is also exactly why you need to start investing now, not when you have a stable job or when the market is less volatile, and not when you are in your 30s or 40s. It's true that some concerns are more long term in nature. For example, saving for retirement is something that takes place over decades.

However, that doesn't make any of your shorter goals, such as saving for a new home and its down payment, any less challenging.

When you have a clear view of your financial milestones, you need to define them and a time when you need to reach them. This way, you don't have to struggle or scramble madly for any of them. Most people out of college or actively in the workforce don't really take a 360-degree view of their financial position and goals.

But it's important to have a short-term as well as a long-term view when it comes to money and savings. The sooner you look at your short-term goals the easier it will be for you to have a good nest egg for retirement.

This also means that starting this process in your 20s and 30s will make it less challenging for you to plan once you move into your 40s, 50s & 60s.

Chapter 3 - Principles of the Wealth Timeline

Stages of Life That Are Directly Linked to the Wealth Timeline

Now that we have a basic idea of what we need to do in order to start building wealth, let's take a look at the wealth timeline.

This is a detailed look at the various stages of building wealth starting from your 20s. We will provide an overview in this chapter and go into detail in the chapters following based on age.

1. New Grad, Stepping into the Workforce

At this point, you need to break down your income and create a budget. Never spend more than your allotted budget on your expenses and you will have taken your first step to building wealth.

This is how you create your budget:
- Keep close track of all your expenses.
  - Use online aggregators such as ClarityMoney.com or Mint.com that will help give you a snapshot of exactly where you need to channel your money and other trends in finances such as how your investments are doing, etc.

- These platforms work really well because they can pull data from your accounts in real-time and you can easily organize them into buckets like food, gas and more.
- Clarity Money even takes this a step further by aggregating your subscriptions and canceling ones that don't add value to your life. I've used it to shave off a few hundred from my monthly bills!
- You can get our FREE monthly budget sheet right here at any time - **bit.ly/bwbudgetsheet**
- This information will give you a better idea about where you stand and will help you make smart choices when it comes to achieving more challenging goals.

Once you've gained control of your budget, it's time to complete a few more goals. These include:

- Pay down all your credit card debts.
  - This is even more important than paying your student loan debt. Interest is a silent killer.
  - The faster you can pay off credit card balances the better. Focus efforts on

paying credit cards with the highest interest rates first. This will save you on high-interest bearing accounts.

○ Another option is leveraging a balance transfer credit card with a lower rate. You can easily perform an online search for "balance transfer credit cards" with lower interest rates.

○ Then, transfer your high-interest accounts to the affordable credit card options available with a MUCH lower rate.

- Start saving for retirement.
  ○ If your employer matches your contributions, match what they offer in a 401(k) or 403(b).
  ○ Consider starting a Roth IRA investment on your own. This can be done easily at the following:
    - etrade.com
    - charlesschwab.com
  ○ If you're not comfortable performing these actions online, these sites have a customer service line AND free financial advisors that can point you in the right direction.
- Designate beneficiaries on all of your financial accounts.

- A beneficiary acts as the benefactor on your accounts should something happen to you. This is CRUCIAL and can be completed easily by contacting customer service at your investment accounts.
- Begin your estate planning.
  - In your 20s, you are most likely NOT thinking about where your funds, savings and investments would go if something were to happen to you, but it's always a good idea to start planning your estate, especially as you start to save and increase your net worth. Estate planning can be completed by contacting a local attorney who can walk you through the process and set up your distributions once you've moved on.
- Get disability insurance.
  - Disability insurance provides short-term benefits to eligible workers who have a full or partial loss of wages due to a non-work-related illness, injury, or pregnancy. This is good to have in the case you're not able to work for a period of time.

2. Moving Forward in Your Career

When you are nearing your 30s, you should have more money coming into your account and the potential to save much more than you did when you were in your early 20s. Some of the things you should be focusing on at this point include:

- If you are in the process of switching jobs, make sure you negotiate an increased salary and leverage your retirement account.
  - The sooner you start to earn the more you will end up having later in life.
  - Take your 401(k) or 403(b) money along with you when you move from one job to another. You have the option to move this into an IRA that you control at any brokerage firm of your choice, or you can roll the money into the new employer's 401(k) plan.

Pro Tip: Start working with a financial planner on a fee-based model. This will help you stay focused on your retirement savings. When you have a professional in the field explaining and showing you how to focus on long-term savings, it's more effective in helping you save money.

3. Getting Married

This is the stage at which your responsibilities increase and you need to make a more concerted effort to save for retirement as well as build wealth. Some of the steps you need to take to ensure you are financially stable include:

- Creating your will or updating the one you have.
- Setting up a healthcare proxy, power of attorney, etc. Many people update these to include their spouse.
- Reevaluate all of your insurance policies and consider getting life insurance.
  - Some couples choose to get their life insurance policies soon after marriage, while some prefer to wait until after their children are born. This depends entirely on your predilection and situation.
  - Consider getting group term insurance. This will provide you cover for a specific period of time through your employer. For additional coverage, however, you'd have to purchase your own individual term insurance.
  - You can also check whether, through marriage, two health insurance policies

will be available to you and what the term will be. Compare these to determine whether it makes much more sense for you and your spouse to be on one policy.

Make it a point to reevaluate whether your disability insurance coverage is adequate.

4. Buying a Home

- While everyone has some idea about how their dream home should be, we don't live in a world where everything will fall in line as we expect it to. It also means that your financial situation may not align perfectly with your goal to buy a home of a certain size in a specific neighborhood.
- One of the best ways to make sure you don't stretch your assets too much is to ensure that you buy a house that doesn't burn a hole in your pocket.

According to The Balance, Lenders typically want no more than 28% of your gross (i.e., before tax) monthly income to go toward your housing expenses, including your mortgage payment, property taxes, and insurance. Once you add in monthly payments on other debt, the total shouldn't exceed 36% of your gross income.[8]

It's never a good idea to overextend. Working with a mortgage broker as well as an investment advisor will help ensure that you invest in a home that allows you to balance your income and debts comfortably.

Other things to consider:

- If you are already married but have not purchased life insurance, NOW is the time to look into it.
- Also, update your disability insurance and make sure the policy would comfortably cover the cost of your new home.

5. Having Kids

As you move towards your 40s, your responsibilities may increase. This is especially true when you have children.

At this point, there are specific steps you need to take in order to provide for them as well as keep your future secure. Some of the items you need to complete include:

- If you don't have a will, it's time you completed one.

- Work with a licensed and experienced attorney and review your estate plan. It's important to make sure that you protect against incapacity and that your assets are well protected.
- If your assets are substantial, establish a trust. If you choose to leave these assets to your children, make sure they aren't immediately payable after your passing.
- Think of a trust as a way to pass your assets (investments, real estate, belongings) to a beneficiary for specified access. Trusts can save beneficiaries from paying fees like real estate taxes and court fees. Thus ,protecting assets from beneficiaries creditors or losses via divorce settlement.
- This is also the time to start saving for your children's college education.
- One of the best ways to do this is to set up automatic transfers by opening a 529 account.

The SEC explains that a 529 plan is a tax-advantaged savings plan designed to encourage saving for future education costs. 529 plans, legally known as "qualified tuition plans," are sponsored by states, state agencies, or educational institutions and are authorized by Section 529 of the Internal Revenue Code.[9]

If at this point your finances do not give you the scope to launch a 529 account, saving for retirement should always be the higher priority.

Your children can work on securing scholarships, take out partial student loans, or choose alternate education as an option. There are dozens of great paying career choices where low-cost online courses in web development, coding and other revenue generating careers can be lucrative. Entrepreneurship as a career path, or studying a trade (electrician, HVAC technician, dental hygienist...) with affordable tuition fees, but you won't be able to do so for retirement.

If you choose to save for their higher education over your own retirement, eventually they may have to support you later in life.

6. Established in Your Career

"I had to make my own living and my own opportunity. But I made it! Don't sit down and wait for the opportunities to come. Get up and make them." – Madam C.J. Walker

When you are in your 40s and 50s, you're probably earning the most of what you'll earn in your life. It's also the time when you need to take a more serious look at your retirement funds and determine whether you are doing all you can to pad them well.

Some things you should be doing at this point include:

- Maxing out all your retirement contributions.
  - Save as much as possible in your traditional IRA or Roth IRA as well as your employer-sponsored retirement account. Maxing out your retirement stems from a few factors. By living beneath your means, budgeting properly and maintaining a modest lifestyle you can contribute a solid amount to retirement.
  - Become more proactive and focused on tax planning.
  - Consult a licensed CPA in order to maximize your deductions. Deductions, in a nutshell, lower your taxable income. Items like charitable donations, job expenses and student loan interest can help you pay less taxes on your income. This is important because at this stage you're likely to be forking out the highest taxes.

Sidenote: A tax deduction is a reduction of income that is able to be taxed and is commonly a result of expenses, particularly those incurred to produce additional income. Tax deductions are a form of tax incentives, along with exemptions and credits.

- Consider setting up a health savings account as this allows you to save on your health expenses with your money.
  - In addition, it also potentially allows you to use this money as an effective investment vehicle.
  - Keeping your tax liabilities in view, determine what your investment choices are. You may want to consider taking additional risk in Roth IRA or Roth 401(k), as you won't pay any taxes on the earnings from those investments.

If you are also caring for your parents and need to keep their needs in mind, do so while setting up your own financial priorities.

Assisted living facilities and home healthcare can both be quite expensive and you need to weigh the costs of these against saving for your children's college education and, more importantly, for your own retirement.

If you have siblings, talk with them about your parents' care needs and try to find a solution that works well for all of you.

7. Take Your Long-Term Care Plans into Account

This is another important milestone you should be considering. Take a look at what you can do so that you are not a burden on your family. Conduct some research into conventional long-term care insurance that also includes personal care, home health care, or nursing home care for individuals over 65 who require supervision.

Because many find this kind of long-term care insurance quite expensive, they don't think of buying it when they are in their 50s. Incidentally, this is also the time when they're facing the financial challenges of retirement, but it doesn't always become possible for them to invest this kind of money at that point of time, and they drop the thought of buying expensive insurance, which they aren't certain they would use.

One suitable solution to this quandary is hybrid policies; these typically offer life insurance with an add-on of a long-term care option.

However, these aren't suitable for everyone because they involve a significant upfront investment. This is also why they become more suitable as an estate-planning tool for many.

8. Start Planning Income for Your Retirement

Most people work their entire lives, accumulate and build their assets. However, they don't have a solid plan in place on the way to retirement for how to maintain stable income. It is extremely important to transition from the accumulation mindset to one where you start looking at de-accumulation. Some steps to take include:

At this stage, you need to have a detailed discussion with your financial planner about the best way to turn your Social Security, IRA, pensions, 401(k), etc. into stable income.

You should consider purchasing an annuity; in this you would use a major portion of your retirement savings to buy a guaranteed source of income for yourself, for a specific time frame.

What is an annuity?

An annuity breaks down your investments into a series of payments made at equal intervals. These can include normal deposits to a savings account, monthly home mortgage payments, monthly insurance payments and pension payments.

This will help you manage your budget and avoid overspending.

Understand how the age at which you decide to take Social Security will impact the amount you receive.

It is also important to learn how to pull your money from various retirement accounts as well as retirement income distributions without actually getting hit with humongous tax bills.

At this age, many people get financial advice from an RICP (Retirement Income Certified Professional).

These financial planners help individuals turn their retirement assets into solid income. They are able to look at various crucial financial factors and provide advice on the best investment options for you. If required, catch up on your retirement contributions to your 401(k) and IRA.

9. Retirement

Well before you retire, it's important that you know what your overall expenses and income are projected to be. At this point, your objective should be to turn your assets into a stable income in a very tax-efficient manner. You can do this by working with your planner and reviewing your plan for the future. It's also important to discuss when the best time would be for you to begin accepting Social Security.

Conduct a Detailed Review of Your Investments

Review what your risk tolerance is with reference to maintaining the nest egg that you have built. This will help you avoid suffering a major loss right when you start on your retirement. Determine what the optimal ways will be to invest your retirement savings in order to ensure that you don't end up outliving it.

Make sure you downsize. A small home can go a long way in helping you reduce the property taxes you pay as well as various expenses such as utilities and more. When you move into a new community, the migration can also have certain social benefits.

Based on your circumstances and situation, you might want to consider relocating to a full retirement community. Today, there are many homes that accommodate independent living. They offer a variety of activities and have options such as full-time care and assistance too.

Be Prudent with Your Investment Choices

"Whatever we believe about ourselves and our ability comes true for us." – Susan L. Taylor, journalist

You also need to consider how you will be able to find potential long-term care costs. If you have not purchased a policy in the past, you could sign up for a hybrid policy now, find some other options for self-funding or sign up for long-term care.

It is important not to make any hasty changes and work with a licensed and trusted advisor. This can help ensure that your retirement plan stays on track. If you have any proceeds from life insurance, invest those based on what your current goals are.

If you have developed an estate plan in the past, work with an experienced attorney, revisit and update the plan as required. In the event that you are incapacitated, a family member can step in to make financial and medical decisions for you. Ensure that the assets will pass on to your family exactly the way you intended them to.

As you can see, building a nest egg for a comfortable retirement is about taking every step with care, weighing your options and making smart investment choices. Starting when you are in your 20s gives you the time you need to do this in a detailed and planned manner. In the forthcoming chapters, we will be taking a closer look at every stage of the wealth timeline.

Chapter 4 - How to Start Saving with $1 at Age 18

"Success is to be measured not so much by the position that one has reached in life as by the obstacles which he has overcome while trying to succeed." – Booker T. Washington

While most youngsters today are quite money conscious, occasionally setting aside some portion of your earnings as a teenager isn't sufficient when it comes to savings. It takes more planning than that to make sure you get into a habit.

When you're 18, savings aren't the first things that come to mind and a retirement fund seems like an almost alien concept. But the fact is that with every passing decade of your life, your financial priorities will change. Your short and long-term financial goals should, in fact, transition along with your situation and circumstances to serve your most crucial needs.

Save Today for a Stable Tomorrow

Today's low interest rates do not really encourage saving. However, that doesn't mean you need to ignore it. When you have some money set aside, it helps you deal with unexpected expenses. Saving money means you end up spending less than you earn and when you eventually have to make any make major purchases, you'll be happy that you have some money set aside for them.

Saving money as a teenager can be quite challenging, especially if your friends are going on weekend trips or splurging on new clothes but it isn't impossible. Once you move into your 20s, you will naturally start thinking about your future, but why not start on the saving habit while you are in your teens?

This is the time when you need to ask yourself whether you are really financially responsible and understand how to move forward with saving money consistently. If you have answered yes to this question, it means you are on the right track. However, if your answer is no, you don't really need to stress. You can start saving now and still have plenty of time to create substantial savings in the forthcoming years.

Regardless of whether you are actively saving, have a bank account and have begun investing in your future, you will need to be patient and put in some effort in order to build your confidence about the financial decisions you make.

Where the Problem Lies

Why is it that so many teenagers don't really have a bank balance to talk about? The answer to this is simple; most youngsters don't give thought to it and a large percentage of them aren't in the habit of saving any money at all.

According to Marketing Charts, both average-income and upper-income teens allocate 60% of their spending to apparel/accessories/shoes and food, with upper-income teens skewing slightly more towards food spending.[10]

There are numerous reasons for this—while some do not bother to set up a savings account, others don't believe that there is an urgent need to do so.

However, in many cases, young people don't set aside any money for savings because they feel they don't have enough money for it in the first place. When you end up spending everything that you earn, it is impossible to save. Once you near the end of the month, you will find that there is nothing left over that you can save. It's also why this effort gets pushed to the next month and the one after that and so on...

How to Break the Cycle

One of the biggest advantages to being young, with reference to saving money, is that you have time on your side. This is a luxury you don't have once you become older. When you start early, you will find that it's much less of an effort to build up a substantial amount for later in life.

Here Are Some Tips to Keep in View:

- Before you spend anything, save some money. Whenever you receive money from different sources, put at least 20% of it into savings before you start to spend on various things.

Why 20%?

The 50/20/30 Rule was made popular by U.S. Senator Elizabeth Warren and her daughter Amelia Warren Tyagi. They introduced this concept in the co-written book *All Your Worth: The Ultimate Lifetime Money Plan* as a good strategy to help people manage their expenses, save money, and still have cash for leisure spending. It breaks your spending down into three buckets:

1. Needs - the bills you need to survive including mortgage, rent, car payment, groceries, etc....
2. Wants - dinner, vacations, Internet, Netflix, etc....
3. Savings - IRAs, emergency savings, etc....

- If you are still living with your parents, or if your daily needs are being met by someone, it's best to set aside a larger portion of your disposable income as savings.

- Investments and savings started at an early age will reap higher rewards compared to if you start decades down the line.

- If possible, work out a certain deal with your parents where they can match your savings. This means, if you set aside $30 from your weekly paycheck, your guardians/parents/grandparents will give you $30 more to add to your savings. It isn't uncommon for many parents to give their kids money for the future. This is especially the case if the money is deposited in an account that can only be accessed later on.

- It's important to consider the opportunity costs for all the purchases you make. Compound growth is a vital aspect of any investment. You can use the power of interest, reinvestment, and dividends as well as conservatively-invested savings to easily double or even triple the amount in 10 years. In some cases (depending on where you invest your money), it can multiply by 10 times in a matter of 30 years!

How Does Compounding Work?

As you know, the bank pays interest on your savings account. You'll see a transaction for the interest payment, and your bank account increases. With compounding interest, you earn interest on the money you deposit and on the interest you already earned—so you earn interest on interest. It's like a double-dipped chocolate sundae.

Now imagine the compounding that happens when you start saving at 18.

Want to Become a Millionaire? All It Takes Is $1

Many 18-year-olds find that they don't have too much money to set aside each week in savings. But what if we told you that all it takes is $1 to get you going? Most people feel that $1 won't take them far at all, but is that really the case?

Well, it's true that $1 won't get you much these days, but if you decide to set aside this amount every single day, you will find that it can give you a substantial bang for your buck. The simple fact is that small amounts of money can add up over time.

If you are interested in knowing how to save half a million dollars for your retirement, take a look at how putting aside just $1 every day could help you achieve this. The three savings options you have are:

- Put the money in a non-interest bearing account.

- Save it in a money market account/savings account at an interest rate of 1%.
- Invest in exchange-traded funds, which track Standard & Poor's 500 index (think of this as the market benchmark).

Let's take a look at how much $1 would give you if you were to save that amount every single day over your entire adult working life. Assume that you have set aside this money for a period of 50 years (starting at age 18 up to 68):

- In a Savings Account (zero interest) you will have $18,250.
- In a Money Market Account (@ 1.00%) you will have $23,646.19.
- In an ETF – no fees (@11.23%) you will have $698,450.54 (returns are not guaranteed and based on the market).
- In an ETF – with fees (@ 10.79%) you will have $594,407.58.

According to US News, at their core, ETFs are funds – which can be comprised of stocks, bonds, commodities or other assets – that are designed to track a particular index. Like stocks, ETFs trade daily on stock exchanges, their prices fluctuating throughout the day.[11]

It's true that $18,250 seems like a meager sum and it won't really suffice to fund your retirement. However, if you live a frugal life, have low healthcare costs, and your mortgage has been paid off, this amount might be enough to cover about one year of your retirement. Based on your situation, it could also easily fund a post-retirement trip with your spouse.

Also, keep in mind this is at $1 PER DAY.

Save $1 a Day in a Money Market/Savings Account

As per the FDIC (Federal Deposit Insurance Corporation), on average, the money market rate currently stands at 0.08% if the account balance is below $100,000. The savings account rate is much lower and stands at 0.06%. However, some banks such as Synchrony Bank and Ally Bank offer rates that are closer to 1 and 2 percent.

And so, if you are able to set aside $1 a day in a money market/savings account that gives you an interest rate of 1% compounded daily, after 50 years, you'd have $ 23,646 in your account. This is a conservative calculation, presuming that you get an interest rate of only 1%.

However, it is distinctly possible that the interest rates will rise at some point in time within this period. It means that your money has the potential to grow much faster. For example, if you get a return of 2%, then after 50 years you'd have a compound amount of $31,178. At a rate of 3%, this amount would be $41,783.

Saving $1 per Day in an ETF

While it's true that investing in stocks carries higher risks, the returns are also greater. This means the chances of saving a sufficient amount of money for retirement are also higher. After investing $1 per day for 50 years, in an ETF (Exchange Traded Fund) that tracked the S&P 500, you would have an amount of $698,450.

Note- Here we are presuming that you are getting an $11.23% return annually. Also, no fund fees have been calculated in this amount, and the assumption is that you begin investing this amount from day one.

ETFs are typically traded like stocks, and this also means that you have to pay a certain commission every time you sell or buy them. However, there are some investment firms and brokerages such as Vanguard, Charles Schwab, and E-Trade that offer you a commission-free ETF option.

As you can see, even $1 can go a long way, if you are consistent with saving it over the years. Most people have the capacity to save much more than this amount, which also means that cumulatively you will have far more than this amount at retirement.

Don't Delay-Start Small Today

If you are 18 years old, this is the perfect time to start saving. These are some things that can set you on the right track:

1. Set up Your Savings Account

It is crucial that you put all your money for saving into a separate account, aside from the one you use for all your day-to-day expenses and monthly bills. Most banks offer savings accounts and you can get this information from your local bank. Keep in mind that some banks have certain minimum balance requirements for these accounts. So, if you are starting with a very small amount like $10/$20 per month, this is something you would need to check first.

If you can't find a local bank that doesn't have the no-minimum-balance account option, or if you are comfortable with conducting your finances via the Internet, you might want to consider online banking solutions. Companies like Capital One and Ally Bank offer no minimum balance saving accounts that are convenient and very easy to use. You can easily start your account with an opening balance of $10. Some banks even offer incentives for signing up.

2. Set up an Automatic Withdrawal of $10 Per Month

You don't have to start big at all and $10 is all it takes to set up your savings account. Many people shy away from doing this because they feel embarrassed at a small amount. However, if you choose the online option that we just discussed, you don't really have to interact with anyone face-to-face. All you have to do is deposit $10 and then set up the $10/per month automatic withdrawal on the account. This should be set as close as possible to the day on which you get paid.

You will notice that you are still able to manage all your expenses properly. Once you have proof that you are able to save as well as survive, you can slowly up your monthly contribution little by little. Increase this amount by only $5 per month or whatever you find comfortable. Over time, you might even be able to increase this particular amount to much more than that. However, setting up this kind of account will prove to you that saving doesn't have to be an uphill task.

3. IRA

Putting your money into an IRA (Individual Retirement Account) will mean it gathers interest over the years and by the time you are 50, you will be lauding the smart saving sense you had when you were 18. IRAs are an excellent place to park your money. Most young people consider them to be 'retirement' accounts (after all, that's what the name indicates); but they are very good investment accounts, even for teenagers.

In fact, you should also consider investing in a Roth IRA. This is because any income that you earn and store there gets taxed today and not at withdrawal. At that point in time, you are more likely to be in a much higher tax bracket. When your money is in a Roth IRA, it grows in a tax-free manner, which also means it multiplies at a much faster rate. This is especially true if you start when you are 18.

Aim to Be a Millionaire

Focus on being a millionaire; start investing when you are 18 and you will have a considerable amount of money at retirement. Put all your spare change in a cookie jar and deposit all the coins in the bank. Have stringent spending rules for every single dollar you earn.

Start working as early as you can. The sooner you have some income the easier it will be for you to save money. The money you save when you start out young adds up at a rapid pace. The $1 that you save today can help you successfully create a stable financial base for tomorrow.

Chapter 5 - How to Build Wealth in Your 30s

"We all have dreams. In order to make dreams come into reality, it takes an awful lot of determination, dedication, self-discipline and effort." — Jesse Owens, world record-setting Olympic athlete

For most people in their 20s, fun, frolic, and spending money as it comes is the norm, but as they move into their 30s, there is a realization for tighter control on the wallet. It is also the time when many people marry and start families.

Your peak earning years are also staring you in the eye. Your career path is on course and you feel confident in a steady, well-growing flow of income. All in all, you start to feel the need to review your finances.

You feel the urgency to ensure that the money you earn is saved and invested to create wealth, so that you have a cushion for your retirement and other future needs. More importantly, you are young and willing to wait for the fruits of your present investment to mature.

The Big Picture

Any average person in their 30s will have stars in their eyes and will dream of living a relaxed life when they are 60 with enough wealth created in the interim 30 years. No two individuals are the same when it comes to setting goals for future investments, especially when planning for a longer horizon of 30 years.

We all would like to optimize investments over that period, but the mix of investments may differ. Most young people in their 30s want an answer to a very relevant question:, "What are the most important investment avenues for me at this juncture?" Before seeking an answer to this query, remember the caveats:

- The focus on short-term investments in the stock market is more of a "get rich quick" concept. This isn't the right way to start investing in your 30's because you cannot time the market and have no control over how it will swing. There are a number of variables in play in this landscape that can make the market extremely volatile and unpredictable.

This makes investing in stocks quite a risky proposition. While you can have a robust mix of investments that also includes stocks and bonds, these should be only one slice of your investment pie.

- Your investments must match your present income flow. It means that without a substantial surplus (which very few professionals can garner), you might not be able to afford to invest in real estate or startups that look promising ... yet.

- You need to search for investment options that are reliable, manageable and accessible to get set on a steady investment path that gives you a stable income 30 years down the line.

Avenues For Building Wealth In Your 30s

In order to get a good start and a firm grip on your finances during your prime (between 30 and 40 years), consider some of these investment paths to tread on, so that you have a very steady footing to bank on as you advance in age.

1. 401(K) Contributions Are Important

If you are working at a company that offers 401(k), which is a pre-tax preferred retirement investment vehicle, try to match your employee's employer's contribution. The higher your contribution, the greater will be the benefit derived when you leave the job post-retirement.

The employer's contribution and the compounded interest it earns is free money for you and this becomes available to you during retirement. In addition to the regular amount, you can also up your contribution when you have some surplus income, such as when you get a raise or when a bonus comes in.

You can also consider the "auto increase" option. This is an online method to increase the percentage of your contribution at a specific frequency. Since this becomes a regular auto-deduction, it systematically increases your contribution over the years. Eventually, the cumulative amount can turn into a tidy sum that can come in handy once you retire.

2. Explore And and Open Additional Retirement Accounts

Paying your 401(k) contributions is only one part of the retirement funds you need to enjoy a comfortable life, but stopping there may not take care of your future. Those who have the foresight and to recognize the changing retirement scenario search for alternative retirement savings accounts. Traditional IRA, Roth IRA and Health Savings Accounts are useful to cover the gap in your retirement funds.

Retirement consultants recommend that you follow the ground rule of saving three times your salary by the age of 40 if you want to retire by around the age of 67. You will need to keep a constant track of your retirement accounts to reach that goal.

3. Put Small Savings To Work

When you want to create wealth, you need to think of investing and adopt a highly focused approach to it. An investment can be as small as $100. Simply put, to be an investor, you do not need a lot of money. You can start with small surplus funds that you have in your savings account. The use of micro-investment apps has become a popular option for small investors.

Among the better known micro-investment apps are platforms such as Acorns, Stash, and Robinhood. These apps aim at simplifying the saving process and allow users to save and invest money in bits and pieces. When a user connects a debit card to the app, it rounds up their purchases to the dollar and makes an automatic transfer. Over the years, these small deposits prove to be a substantial amount. You can learn more about these apps by visiting **bit.ly/awesomeinvestmentapps**.

Apart from these apps, a savvy investor can also consider mutual funds to invest money when they get the opportunity to set aside some funds. Warren Buffett, the investment Guruguru, suggests low-cost-index funds as a good investment avenue.

4. Future Purchases Need Additional Savings

As an adult, your desires soar; you start to look at your future needs and how to meet them. You may think of purchasing a home, create a travel plan or opt to enroll for grad school or a particular trade. These and other purchase ideas would need you to set aside some savings with regularity. All of these goals will have different time frames with expenses spread over a period of time. You will need to tailor your saving strategy and factor in these expenses into your plans for wealth creation.

5. Create a Safety Net

Having an investment strategy in place is a precaution and preparation to meet your future needs, but it doesn't help prevent eventualities. Life can sometimes throw unpleasant surprises. Losing a job can be an unforeseen event, as can a medical emergency or temporary disability due to an accident.

You need a good financial cushion to meet the challenges of these unpredictable life events. It's also why you need to think of a Rainy Day Fund or an Emergency Fund. It can save you from the hiccups that have the potential to derail your other goals.

So, how much should your Rainy Day Fund corpus be? There is no one-size-fits-all answer to this question.

Individual situations differ, but experts explain that you should maintain at least three to six 3-6 months' worth of savings separately as an Emergency Fund. This fund needs to be liquid so as to be available on demand. You can consider stashing these savings in a high-yielding savings account, stocks, bonds, etc. that can be accessed easily, when you need them.

Do Not Lose Sight of Major Goals

"If you have no confidence in self, you are twice defeated in the race of life." – Marcus Garvey

If you want to build wealth, you must be clear about the financial goals you have set for yourself in your 30s and the steps you need to follow to reach them. However, goals are not written in stone and the mix of goals may change over time. This also means the strategies to achieve them may need intermittent tweaking. A time-bound review and update of your goals is a prerequisite for wealth creation.

The 30s is an essential starting point to build a sound foundation for your retirement. However, there are some expenses hurdles that you need to navigate on your path to retirement. These are inevitable and every person finds themselves faced with certain major expenses, especially if they are married and have a family. For instance, you may like to spend on your children's weddings or on their higher education to give them a boost on their career path. These may be necessary expenses, but they are also detractions that can create roadblocks in meeting the goals you have set for retirement. You may need to find ways and means to meet these needs without disturbing the key elements of your retirement plan.

The secret to building wealth in the your 30s is to start saving as early as you can to benefit from the concept we discussed in earlier chapters called compounding. This works silently but is very effective over a longer period of time as the interest over interest accumulates. It has a snowball effect that makes your retirement funds swell to a level you could never have imagined to be possible.

A Few Precautions

The goals set for wealth building need to be guarded like a hawk. It's a nest egg and you need to balance the temptation to spend now, with the creation of wealth in the future. In the interim period, you may change your job, but you cannot leave your retirement savings behind, even at the cost of paying higher fees. You can even consolidate multiple retirement accounts that you have opened, to save costs.

Building wealth is a mission that needs you to remain steadfast. Your goals set your priorities. You'll need to guard against debts that limit your ability to meet your retirement and other saving goals. You may need to follow the golden rule -"income minus savings is consumption" to stay on track with building wealth in your 30s. As time passes, try to diversify your income by investing in stocks and home equity with your discretionary income.

And to achieve all this, engage actively in financial education to know and understand what you aren't aware of and what you are unable to comprehend. The path to financial prosperity lies in choosing your destination, knowing where you are and facing the challenges to reach financial freedom. You got this.

Chapter 6 - How to Build Wealth in Your 40s

"You can only become accomplished at something you love. Don't make money your goal. Instead pursue the things you love doing and then do them so well that people can't take their eyes off you." – Maya Angelou (African American author and poet)

Building wealth is not a race.

As the late, great Nipsey Hussle would say:
"The Marathon Continues."

Wealth is a marathon unless you're a highly successful techie or made resounding success at your first startup, joining the millionaire or billionaire club at a very young age. For most of us it's an uphill road.

So, how does an average person in their 40s handle the building of wealth at this stage in life? It's different when you're in your 20s; you rarely think of money and finance at that age. In your 30s, you start to get serious about earning and saving. You feel the need to think about life during retirement and how to provide for it.

Time to Get Your Finances on Track

But when you hit your 40s, you are in the middle of your life before retirement. It is that point at which the thoughts of building wealth begin to mature and take concrete shape. This is the stage when you feel the need to take stock of your financial situation and look at your performance in achieving the wealth-building goals you set for yourself in your 30s.

You may largely be free of the credit-card-debt cycle; a major portion of your house mortgage payment and similar financial obligations could be decreasing. Your career path is clear and you are at the peak of your earning cycle. Now you want to ensure that you are on track to growing wealth and reaching your goal.

In case you find that you are a little off track, this is the time to work out the correctional steps you need to take to get things right. If you find that your plans have worked, you may adopt a more aggressive approach and scale up your goals too. Here are some tips to keep your wealth-building exercise energized.

1. Revisit Retirement Plans

The wealth-building retirement plans that you started in your 30s have been active for almost a decade and this is the time to revisit them. If you find that you have crossed the milestones successfully, it is an indication that you have the potential to set higher goals and reach them. It means that you should continue with your present retirement plan contributions. You can also search for new retirement savings options or add to the present ones.

2. Seeking New Opportunities

When you get ready to increase additional savings, it's good to diversify avenues that are not related to employer-sponsored plans. Traditional IRAs or a Roth IRA are good investment options that provide some benefits. IRAs come with tax advantages. A Roth plan does not require you to pay taxes on account earnings, but there are income limits that decide your eligibility to invest. Find plans that are reliable and stable and provide long-term gains.

3. Retirement Savings - A Priority

You need to remind yourself that retirement savings are a priority that cannot be sacrificed to meet other demands. Your 40s are a period when you are likely to start relaxing your efforts about retirement income plans. You are likely to lose sight of retirement savings as a priority whenever demands for huge funds for your kids' education eclipse everything else.

In fact, most parents start an education fund for their children when the kids are in diapers. But if you have been lax about your responsibility, you will have to find the extra money by doing some consultancy work or taking up side gigs when possible. This new dimension to your working life will set the groundwork for you to work when you retire, helping you earn some additional income and keeping you active.

Note - we've curated a list of side hustles you can take up in your free time. Just visit **bit.ly/sidehustlebible** for details.

But you should never allow your retirement plans to be derailed by these demands. You can always find options to reduce education expenses and make it more affordable. While funding your children's higher education, you may find yourself with empty coffers later in life. This also means you need to balance the responsibility towards your family now with your needs post-retirement.

It is crucial for you to protect your nest egg. After all, your kids can always accumulate scholarships, take education loans to fund their college education, or take up trades that afford a very feasible option for children who aren't interested in a traditional four-year university. College isn't for everyone and there are a lot of alternatives.

Otherwise, you could consider partially funding your children's education so that you are able to strike a balance and not upset the balance, so to speak.

4. Systemizing Investments

By the time you hit your mid-40s, you have a fairly good idea of your income flows, retirement investments and other assets that you have built over the years. Take a holistic view of all your investments and the returns earned on them. It could be possible that you have changed your job and forgotten about your old 401(k) and any other benefits that you have accrued.

You will need to reinvest in its entirety into a new retirement investment plan, without diverting the funds to meet some other expenses.

You need to look at asset allocation and diversifying investments to maximize returns. When you are in your 40s, you can take some risk with the surplus money in your pocket and start investing in stocks, mutual funds, and bonds.

Equity investments generally provide good returns in the longer term and give a good boost to your broader investment earnings. They carry higher risks but give higher rewards too, if invested prudently. If you find it difficult to handle your investing, do not shy away from seeking professional help. The idea is to find avenues that will provide a good return on investment within a comparatively shorter time span. An experienced financial consultant can give you some solid advice and point you in the right direction.

The dividends earned from these investments contribute to passive income that is earned year after year as you remain invested; but it is prudent to consider a growth option when you are in your 40s rather than a dividend option as you are likely to splurge the extra money earned.

Finance experts consider balancing equity investment with some investment in debt like bonds as a desirable option. Be flexible and reallocate funds from one investment to another if it has lost its attractiveness in terms of appreciation and returns.

5. Invest in Wealth-Creating Assets

Wealth building is spread over generations and the legacy of wealth left behind by a generation is the building block for the next one.

Wealth helps to build wealth.

Today, people of color in their 40s have the responsibility of creating wealth because we can tap into the opportunities for higher income earning opportunities like tech jobs and startups that result in a wider job force and more opportunities for growth.

The extra income earned needs to be diverted into solid asset-building avenues such as home equity, the cornerstone of generational wealth. If the realty investment is in rental property, it will boost your retirement income significantly.

6. Get Life Insurance Cover

Life insurance is a risk cover and needs to be looked at from a different perspective. When you buy a life insurance policy, you ensure that the nest egg you have built for retirement remains intact for others in the event of your death. The retirement money will not be used for your burial expenses or paying off your debts.

A whole life policy is a good option to build cash value but needs to be considered carefully in terms of higher premium costs compared to the returns on investment. When the policy matures during your lifetime, the funds are available for investment.

Talk to a life insurance provider for details on how to get started.

7. Account and Limit Your Expenses

"Many people don't focus enough on execution. If you make a commitment to get something done, you need to follow through on that commitment." – Kenneth Chenault

Wealth building can occur only when you aggressively wield an axe on expenses that are not budgeted. It is important to regularly examine your income, savings and expenses by using technology-enabled tools. Keep a check on income-draining expenses such as big ticket items, luxury travel, and overuse of credit cards and personal loans. You will be amazed by the saved income generated by setting budgets and limits for these major expenses.

This is critical because your earnings are likely to be higher during your 40s, which can lead you to relax your hold on your purse strings; but this is the best opportunity to build wealth through savings and investments, as well as purchasing income-earning assets. Knowing that money creates money and that it has alternative uses is the key to wealth building; taking calculated investment risks and balancing that out with prudent spending is the best way to ensure that you have a comfortable cushion to fall back on, while building wealth too.

In Sum…

This is the dream phase of your life when you are full of energy and enthusiasm to accept change and face challenges.

You might have lofty intentions but could suffer from poor execution. For this reason alone, your focus on earnings must remain at the center of all your activities.

This is a time to match the leap in earnings with a leap in savings and investment. The tendency to treat savings and investment as residuals after meeting all justified and unjustified expenses is no less than catastrophic for wealth building.

Here are some simple rules to follow:

- Rein in expenses.
- Eliminate debts and loans to stem undue leakages from your income stream.
- Review your savings and investments at regular intervals by putting in place automated systems.
- Realign investment avenues, if necessary, to maximize your returns.
- You need to adopt an aggressive approach to wealth building while pursuing your career and professional goals all the while providing a comfortable life for you and your family.

Do not make wealth building a secret or isolated project.

When you make your family members understand your income, expenses, saving and wealth building dynamics, all of them will be encouraged to help you make your retirement plans a success years down the track. After all, this is something that will benefit them as well as future generations too. This kind of a concerted effort can go a long way in making your dream of bolstering your wealth a reality.

Chapter 7 - How to Build Wealth in Your 50s

"Never be limited by other people's limited imaginations." – Dr. Mae Jemison, first African American female astronaut

Crossing five decades of your life is considered a big milestone for various reasons. You have journeyed a long way since you started earning and enjoying the independence that accompanied it.

When you touch 50, the moment of awakening arrives and you start giving serious thought to how you can save some more of your earnings for retirement and build wealth for future generations.

Looking Back

You reached your 30s and someone whispered the word "retirement" in your ear. If your employer provided for it, you joined the 401(k) bandwagon. But as family responsibilities started piling on your shoulders, the balancing act between income, expenses and saving may have left you floundering to stay afloat.

But you continued to persist and scaled higher financial peaks in your career, set new goals and worked to meet them. In spite of this, your retirement savings might have been sidetracked for a while until you crossed 40 years of age. By the time you reached 50, you were more settled and had a financial cushion; the thought of retirement wasn't all encompassing.

But once you cross this half a century milestone, the worries of retirement start to resurface. You suddenly start to feel that ten years is not enough to make good all the gaps created in savings and investment to meet your retirement needs. Of course, you have given some thought to retirement and its requirements and planned for it by setting goals over the years.

But with providing for and managing all the regular and sudden expenses, you might have faltered along the way and found some excuses to miss the targets for savings, investment and wealth building. Now it's time to speed up your efforts and run the marathon to reach your retirement destination on time.

Why Your 50s Are So Important

There are opportunities to seize and challenges to face in your 50s. You may be largely free from major family responsibilities such as children's education, mortgage payments towards your home, and car loans. Now you feel the need to look at your approach to life and especially towards your finances.

The major reason is that when you hit 60 (retirement age), the regular flow of monthly income suddenly evaporates. You need to open the so-far-untouched tap of savings and investments. But is the resource tank properly filled to provide you a constant flow without depletion?

You now feel the urgency to run a complete check on your portfolio of savings and investments, your debts and any other payments owed by you. You want to undertake the exercise of determining your net worth, an indicator of your wealth generation and wealth building.

If you find that your net worth is healthy, you can vigorously add new retirement plans. On the other hand, if it isn't as robust as you expected it to be, corrective measures will need to be taken in a hurry. Your goal is to make your retirement a period that energizes you to work on passion projects, enjoy, and relax. Here are some guidelines for critical thinking and the crucial steps necessary to build wealth in your 50s.

Retirement Benchmarks

You need to use this important 10-year period to create a more solid foundation for your retirement income. Even more importantly, the steps you take today will also decide whether you have any wealth set aside for your future generations. Looking at some benchmarks and putting your own portfolio into proper perspective helps at this juncture. These are some of the things you need to focus on:

- Some financial experts suggest that by your 50s, you should have six times your salary[12] saved in various components of your portfolio. It means that if your annual earning was $70,000, your saving should be between $ 280,000 and $420,000.

- Some use a different approach based on individual expectations about retired life and the income stream they expect to meet their needs.

- A bucket strategy (that looks at various elements of saving as buckets to be managed) is yet another popular approach to plan for your retirement.

- Using a retirement calculator will give you a better idea of what your income needs to be during retirement, based on different savings and investment scenarios. A quick Google search for the term "retirement calculator" should get the job done.

Wealth Generation in Your 50s- The Steps to Take

There are some basic building blocks to generate wealth in your 50s in addition to the benchmarks or methods you employ. Since the earning capacities of individuals differ, the retirement milestones reached by them for savings and investments may vary.

This also means the capacity to ramp up efforts to save more may vastly differ. But there are some common factors that work like road signs to help you arrive at the destination. Let's take a look at some of them.

1. Pad up Your Retirement Contributions

- All those who enjoy the benefit of 401(K) under the pre-tax employer-sponsored retirement plan will have contributed as much as they can to maximize the employer's contribution. If not, this is the last chance to ramp up your contribution to enjoy the benefit of a sizeable sum at the time of retirement. It is free, tax-deferred money earned from the employer while you were an employee, and every withdrawal attracts a tax.

- Once you reach the maximum limit available to you, you need to supplement it with an IRA. The traditional IRA is a tax deferred account and the withdrawal is taxable. This process of padding your retirement portfolio is advantageous. Whether you are 50 or above, the IRS permits you to divert an additional $6000 per year to your work retirement plan. This is over and above the $18500 contribution limit for 2018. You can decide which vehicle you want to invest in and choose a good investment firm to handle your account.

- If you want to leverage all your retirement saving options, you can use a high deductible health insurance plan. The option of an individual plan will allow a saving of $3350 in a health savings account (HSA) and a family plan of $ 6750. At the age of 65, you can withdraw from this account tax-free but with a proviso that it is to meet medical expenses. If not, you will have to pay tax on the withdrawal amount.

2. Roth IRA Option

Roth IRA is a valuable retirement tool for those entering midlife. It's true that for Roth IRA you don't get any tax deduction at the point of investment. But it is advantageous because you do not pay any tax at the point of withdrawal. This provides you with the flexibility to withdraw from the accumulated amounts as you advance in life. Roth IRAs have an additional benefit—if the heirs are the beneficiaries of this amount, it has a softer tax impact for them as well.

3. Empty Debt Baggage

Retirement means you look forward to conclude working or work part time. In short, your regular income flow is halted. This makes it necessary for you to look at your financial obligations that result in debt. Consider it a period to streamline your budget by eliminating debts so that you are completely debt-free by the time you retire.

When you are earning, financial institutions and credit card companies are eager to offer you loans resulting in a debt trap. You might have created debts from property mortgages, car loans and the use of credit cards. These sources of debt can weigh you down during retirement. You need a strategy to pay off all your debts and be as debt-free as possible as you approach retirement.

The golden rule to pare debt is to pay off the debts that carry higher interest rates. Credit card loans have high monthly interest rates and these often prove the costliest. You can reduce the interest by transferring these loans to cards that come with lower interest rates. Pay them off and ensure that you do not create new loans. The same applies to other loans, but prioritize your loan payments and pay them without affecting your retirement savings.

If you have developed a strong social network and a reputation for meeting your obligations, it is useful to take loans at lower interest rates from friends to pay off costly loans. Debts cannot be wished away and they can ruin your best plans to build wealth and need to be handled with urgency and resoluteness. Never be a lone debt warrior. Make sure your family understands how important this aspect is and they will support you in your endeavors.

4. Downsize Your Home

There are a variety of loans, but there are no retirement loans. So if paying a mortgage is proving difficult without affecting retirement savings, it might be time to downsize your home and reduce all expenses including the interest on your mortgage. It is a hard compromise, but the sooner you do it the higher the reward in terms of maintaining an unaffected income flow during retirement. In fact, it's easier to maintain a smaller house too, thus becoming an added advantage before retirement.

5. Diversify and Manage Risk

When you take care of your retirement savings and try to be debt-free, you are assured of a regular income. But this may not help in income growth or wealth building. The latter is possible only when you create assets that increase in value as time passes.

You can achieve this by diverting a major chunk of your growing income during your 50s into stocks, mutual funds and bonds. Equity is now a well-established vehicle for increasing your wealth multifold over a long period of time. Volatility is a feature of the stock market, which keeps many risk-averse investors away from venturing into it.

"But the higher the risk higher the reward" goes a popular saying in the stock market. When you invest some of your surplus funds in stocks of well-managed companies, you are more likely to enjoy significant gains than loss. Some things to keep in mind while investing in the stock market include:

- What you need is correct timing in selecting the right stocks and reviewing their performance at regular intervals.
- You also need to tweak your investments and use a mix of short, medium and long-term strategies to match market trends.
- Alternatively you can invest in prudently managed mutual funds and some bonds to achieve the goal of generating substantial returns in the long run.

If you opt for the services of a financial advisor, keep a tab on their fees as they may corrode your portfolio earnings. Ensure you work with an advisor with proven experience and one who understands what your short and long-term investment objectives and goals are.

Safeguard Your Interests

Some other things you can do when you are in your 50s include:

- Ensure that your asset allocation is conducive to your retirement income flow. It needs to match your requirements and should not heavily tilt in the direction of risk.

- Keep your stock investments at a level where they do not dent your regular income but contribute to it over a longer period.

- The pre-retirement decade is a period to run a complete check on your assets, liabilities, risk-carrying assets, wealth-building assets, dead investments or dead assets. You may have a vacation home or an investment in land that has turned into an income-eroding asset. It is time to convert such toxic assets into cash and invest the money in some income-earning assets.

- Interest rates can drop steadily in the future, posing a challenge to your savings plans. You can meet this challenge by building a much larger and longer-lasting portfolio.

- Be prudent about every dollar you spend and divert as much as possible towards retirement opportunities.

- Postpone retirement, if possible, and cut out some of the frills from your lifestyle (cook vs. eating out, work out at home to forego gym membership, etc.).

In short, all the steps you take during this decade (50s to 60s) should be aimed at restoring your finances to health.

Make Your 50s a Creative Period

Your 50s can be an enjoyable and stress-free period if you have laid a sound foundation for wealth building in your 30s and 40s. You can use this decade to reinforce the existing solid foundation so it carries you through your retirement period effortlessly. Experiment with your surpluses to create a lasting legacy of wealth building for your future generations that many people of color lack.

Take a close look at your retirement money score that reveals the lifestyle your potential future income can sustain. This will be based on three factors: age, salary and retirement savings. Focus on maintaining your health to ensure that your medical expenses don't increase when you are in your 50s.

The Cornerstones of Building Wealth as You Near Retirement

Discipline, budgeting and a thorough review of financial net worth are the keywords for this decade. Account for every dollar now as you enter your 50s. Save and invest it wisely to strengthen your nest egg, bolster your financial security and fill your pockets to enter your 60s for a peaceful and financially secure retirement life.

Keep in mind that it's never too late to step up your game; take stock of your financial situation and make changes that will help you improve it and build wealth.

A decade is a long time and if you start to focus on these aspects when you cross the 50-year milestone, you will still be able to reinforce your financial base within ten years and build some more wealth too.

Chapter 8 - The Steps after Retirement

"If I didn't define myself for myself, I would be crunched into other people's fantasies for me and eaten alive." – Audre Lorde (Caribbean-American poet & author)

Retirement is unchartered territory and a new experience. It's like crossing a border not fully aware of what lies beyond and errors can only make you adapt. It gives you the opportunity to relax and enjoy life as you wish.

But you don't receive a paycheck at the end of the month and you experience the loss of comfort that getting a regular income at regular periods each month can provide. Now you need to dip into the income you derive from your savings and investments accumulated over the years.

The new challenge is to create an income support system until you reach the average retirement age. You also need to ensure there is steady income growth to take care of additional expenses as you advance in age. Once your pension and Social Security payments come on stream, you can partially do away with this bridging arrangement based on your investment portfolio income.

The post-retirement period ushers in twin changes in finance and lifestyle. It takes time to understand the full implications of these changes. A look at the retirement timetable will throw light on how to cope with the changes in the income stream at various intervals of retired life.

The Retirement Timetable

This timetable highlights certain years of your life and their importance from a financial viewpoint in your post-retirement period. It is useful to keep a tab on these landmark years as actionable points as follows:

Age 55

If you retire or happen to lose your job as you turn 55 years of age, you might be eligible to:

- Withdraw from your tax-deferred savings plans without having to pay a 10% penalty, provided you qualify for one of the exceptions mentioned in the federal tax code.
- Get pension benefits from some employer plans, if you have put in the required years of service.

Age 59½

If you do not owe a 10% penalty at the time of retirement, you can generally tap into:

- Your personal tax-deferred savings plans such as IRA and annuities.
- Your employer-sponsored savings plans.

Age 60

You are entitled to receive:
- Social Security benefits, if you are a widow or widower.

Age 62

At this age, your eligibility may cover

- Full pension benefits from your employer, based on the plan.
- Receiving reduced Social Security benefits if you so choose.
- "Reduced" means that the Social Security benefits you receive will be 20 to 30 percent less every month than waiting until full retirement

age. The benefits your spouse receives may be reduced even more. (You can access information about these benefits from The Social Security Administration (SSA))

Age 65

Here are some year-specific conditions to receive full pension and Social Security benefits from most employers:

- If you were born in 1937 or earlier.
- If you are a widow or widower, you can get full Social Security benefits if you were born before January 2, 1940. Your eligibility would depend on the year of your birth if you were born after 1937.
- At 65, you usually become eligible for Medicare benefits too.

Age 66–67

For this age group, too, there are year-specific conditions for receiving Social Security benefits, which include:

- Born between 1943 and 1954 - Entitled to full Social Security benefits at age 66.

- Born between 1955 and 1960 - Social Security benefits increase annually from the age of 66 and two months to age 67.
- Born in 1961 or later – Full retirement age is 67 for full benefits.

Age 70

Mark this age to start collecting your Social Security benefits if you haven't done it. No additional benefit increase is available even if you delay taking benefits.

Age 70½

Age to start withdrawals from:

- Your traditional IRAs but not from Roth IRAs.
- Employer-sponsored retirement plans, such as a 401(k), (unless you're still in employment).

Maximizing your income in the post-retirement period depends on a mix of withdrawals from your retirement plans, the availability of Social Security benefits and income from other investments.

Create a Retirement Budget – The Costs to Include

Most retirees operate in a restricted financial environment. The income flows also remain uncertain and fluctuating. With advancing age, there is also a rapid increase in medical expenses. Both economic and financial conditions can hurt your nest egg.

It is imperative that you prepare your budget and factor in necessities, emergencies, and entertainment. Match this budget with your income flow. This will also help you decide whether you need to cut any corners and, if so, for which items.

How You Spend Money after Retirement

The retirement period will pare your commuting costs as well as various expenses on clothes and eating out. But new expenses may replacc them as you feel the need to spend on healthcare services or new hobbies you take up to make your days enjoyable. These will form an integral part of the budget and should be factored in, based on your specific needs, preferences and interests.

Medicare Premiums

Medicare premium costs are an essential part of any budget. These costs vary depending on the type of plans you buy. Medicare Part A hospital insurance is not something on which people spend their money. However, Medicare Part B medical insurance amounts to a $ 121.80 standard premium for most people while a few specific groups may pay higher premiums.

There are also Medicare Part D prescription drug plans for which the premiums vary depending on the plan selected. A Medigap plan, used to cover some of Medicare's out-of-pocket expenses, can be another addition to the premium you pay.

Tax Payments

You have tax-deferred retirement savings like 401(k) and IRAs. Each withdrawal from these savings is subject to tax. Social Security benefit is also taxable (though partially) if your income crosses a particular limit. You can reduce your tax bill by timing the withdrawals that carry minimum tax payment.

Do Not Cross the Withdrawal Rate

Once you retire, you need to decide what your monthly withdrawal amount will be based on your total savings and your budget that covers all your expenses. Your financial advisor can advise you on how to manage the flow of funds into your retirement portfolio. It's best to maintain your withdrawals as per the budgeted amount.

If you have stocks and mutual funds in your portfolio, you may get some additional income when there is an improvement in market performance. However, even when you enjoy higher returns from your investments, it's best not to splurge all that surplus income. This is because the stock market is always highly volatile and you can never predict when the situation will change and result in a drop in income.

People often make the mistake of overspending and cross their budgeted amount, which can cause them to fall short of funds when necessary. You can also adjust your withdrawal amount for inflation. Whenever you feel the need to increase the withdrawal amount, consult your financial advisor to ensure that you use your retirement funds judiciously.

Earn Some Extra Income

Some people save handsome amounts while they are working and have a good financial cushion during their retirement period. But this isn't the case with everyone and many feel the pinch of not receiving a regular paycheck. These people can benefit from taking up some part-time job or gig. The money they earn will add to their income and put them on more solid financial ground.

If you are able to get a part-time job of your choice, it may add to your happiness index as it also gives you the chance to interact with people for some part of the day. When you retire and stop working altogether, a feeling of emptiness can reside and can give rise to problems like depression that affect your health.

Small jobs like selling products online or doing some work from home keep you physically and mentally engaged for some time. They also provide you the time and money for travel or entertainment. People who have some expertise in a particular industry also find consulting work in the same company or some other establishments in the same field.

Healthcare Expenses Mount

With increasing age come increased medical costs and this also increases the amount of money you spend on Medicare. While you are entitled to certain deductibles under the Medicare Part B, 20% of the remaining Medicare-approved amount is paid by you.

You can supplement traditional Medicare with an additional insurance plan for which you pay an extra premium. Medicare covers certain preventive care services with no out-of-pocket costs. However, this leaves out some commonly needed medical items such as eyeglasses and hearing aids. You need to factor these into your overall medical costs.

Lower Your Food Bills and Stay Healthy

Improving your culinary skills and cooking healthy meals at home is doubly advantageous as it helps keep you healthy and your food expenses under control. However, you may feel tempted to spend time with friends over lunches and dinners. You can save on your food expenses by using coupons at grocery stores and senior discounts at restaurants.

Provision for Emergencies

You might have created an emergency fund before retirement, but you need to continue adding to it. That's the only way you will be able to keep in step with inflation and constantly rising living and other expenses. You can use your emergency fund to cover recurring and unexpected expenses like home repairs, replacement of appliances, etc.

Your nest egg is for regular payments and you should not dip into it for any emergencies. If you do not have an emergency fund, it is advisable to tap into your long-term savings, which have the least tax impact on withdrawal.

Entertainment and Travel

"Passion is energy. Feel the power that comes from focusing on what excites you." – Oprah Winfrey

Retirement is an amazing time for leisure, enjoyment, relaxation and travel. You can always find deals that offer discounts to seniors for movie theatres, museums, and parks. If you feel like taking up a hobby or activity, look for low-cost classes to learn new things that interest you.

Travel can be expensive, but there are ways to make it affordable. You can travel during off-seasons, swap homes or stay with friends. But all said and done, you will need to provide some funds for these activities in your budget because they add to your happiness quotient, which is a very important aspect of living a stress-free and happy life post-retirement.

Grandparents' Favorites

Grandchildren have a special place in the lives of retirees and can change their spending priorities to cater to their loving demands. Some grandparents like to give their grandchildren gifts; others love to travel to see them while some others want to create a trust fund for them. All in all, the thought of grandchildren can bring about changes in the post-retirement budget that you might not have given any thought to during your pre-retirement period.

Leaving Your Footprints

Advancing age makes retirees think of leaving some cash, gifts, heirlooms, jewelry or other valuable things they possess to their children and grandchildren. Many like to provide for these things in their budgets. Some prefer to spell their wishes in their will, while others complete this task during their lifetime. Regardless of the avenue you follow, this too becomes a part of your budget.

Reckless and unplanned spending habits can never make your retirement an enjoyable period. In a way, it is good to ensure that every dollar is stashed carefully to make your retirement period a hassle-free one. Spending your time productively and constructively adds to your personal well-being. If you can manage your time well, you will be able to add a lot of free or low-cost activities to your daily life. These will give you a sense of fulfillment and make living worthwhile.

Retirement is an opportunity to open a new chapter in your life. Add a new opportunity to it with every passing day and find different ways to make this stage of your life a happy one.

Chapter 9 - Barriers to Wealth Building That Black Americans Face

Four centuries have gone by since the first captive Africans arrived at Point Comfort on the James River in Virginia. From slavery to freedom, it is a story of extreme hardship, obstacles, and triumph.

People of color continue to face the challenges of racism and systemic obstacles in building wealth for ourselves and future generations. This is evident in the struggle for equality in economic opportunities and mobility to be on par with White Americans in a free democracy.

Why Is Building Wealth Important?

Wealth is the backbone of the economic well-being of an individual, a family, and a community. Wealthy families have the financial security to meet various commitments like spending on children's education to secure their future, buying a house or meeting unforeseen expenses.

Wealth is also a cushion for periods of joblessness and allows people to take business investment risks to increase wealth. The income earned and accumulated in the pre-retirement period guarantees a secure retired life and helps to leave an inheritance for future generations.

All of this is possible via a lucrative career during your working life. You can save at decent rates of interest, and your loans do not carry the burden of burdensome interest. Your financial well-being is dependent on the basic building blocks of good economic opportunities and unbiased treatment of your savings and debt.

Everyone has different reasons for building wealth. When you have wealth, it ensures you have the money to live a comfortable life and that you are able to splurge on certain luxuries, provide for your family and create generational wealth. But, more importantly, it provides control over your life and gives you the freedom to do the things you enjoy.

The Barriers to Building Wealth

Over generations, Black Americans have been systematically sidelined from the mainstream. When you take a closer look, you realize that there are a number of barriers we face to wealth building. In this chapter, we dissect those barriers, and in the upcoming chapter, we provide actionable solutions.

1. The Racial Wealth Chasm Persists

Racial inequality in wealth-building opportunities has persisted over a long period. This has deprived African Americans of the wealth and status that others enjoy.

Average wealth for White families is seven times higher than average wealth for Black families. Worse still, median White wealth (wealth for the family in the exact middle of the overall distribution—wealthier than half of all families and less wealthy than half) is twelve times higher than median Black wealth.[14]

Median wealth divides all families into two equal parts with 50% above the median and the other below it. Wealth building is minimal in Black families. While less than 10% of White families are without wealth, more than 25% of Black families have zero or negative net worth.[14] This wealth gap has widened over the years making it an arduous task for Black Americans to build wealth (across age, education, income, and occupation level).

2. The Effects of the Wealth Gap

People of color can provide better and higher education to our children only when we have higher savings for investing in education. Educated Blacks can compete for better-paying jobs and economic opportunities.

Wealth is built through savings and investment, which is made possible from higher incomes. Wealth means the ability to invest in a house for a family that acts as an investment for future generations. Higher incomes also result in better mobility to places where high-paying jobs are available.

The unjust and unequal wealth gap has another disturbing angle when you look at the absolute figures.

> While median employed African Americans struggled to assimilate the wealth of $13,460, White American wealth stood at $ 142,180 in 2016.[15] The gap started widening just before the recession of 2007 and increased with every passing year. It's no surprise that Black Americans enter the retirement period with little wealth to live a life of economic well-being.

3. Housing and the Wealth Gap Connect

Home ownership is a significant part of wealth building during one's lifetime and over generations. It accounts for about two-thirds of total wealth for a median household. Therefore, a racial wealth gap is primarily a housing wealth gap.

In addition to employment and wage discrimination, people of color experience significant discrimination in the financial housing market. Over generations, Black Americans with decent incomes have been denied access to the housing market in a very structured way.

Let's Talk about Redlining

The concept of redlining was started by the Home Owners Loan Corp. with maps that were color-coded to indicate where it was safe to insure mortgages. Any locations where African Americans lived nearby were colored red to indicate to appraisers that these neighborhoods were too risky to insure mortgages.

This concept was picked up by the Federal Housing Administration and then adopted by the Veterans Administration.

Housing policies were rife with redlining and restrictive covenants, preventing people of color from acquiring land, either for building houses or for investment. There was discrimination in the housing loan sector as well, making it almost impossible for Black Americans to build home equity, and this further widened the wealth gap.

Even today, these racial and ethnic disparities loom large in the homeownership rate among millennials.

From 1999 to 2015, young, White adults in the 18 to 34 age range had a homeownership rate of 42%. This was the highest of any ethnic/racial group. In comparison, only 18% African American young adults were homeowners.[16]

Having well-heeled parents who are homeowners considerably ups the chances of a young adult being a homeowner themselves.

This is primarily because parents who own real estate are able to imprint upon their children's minds the importance of being a homeowner. They are also in a better position to help their children with the nitty-gritty of house financing and purchase. Many wealthy parents may also lend their adult children a hand with down payments for their home purchase.

The effects of this are seen in the racial ownership gap because Black parents have a homeownership rate that is 35% lower than their White counterparts.

4. Black American Unemployment Rates Rise

The housing bubble that contributed to the recession of 2007 also engulfed African Americans. Due to discriminatory policies, people of color were the victims of predatory, high interest and high-leverage mortgages and when the housing bubble burst, that became another burden.

In the post-recession period, Black unemployment rates zoomed to double that of White unemployment rates. Its impact was seen in higher delinquency and foreclosure rates in loans taken by people of color. The American economy was recovering at a very sluggish pace and that only added to the woes of the Black community in the country.

Even though housing prices did ultimately recover, the rates proved to be disadvantageous for people of color. The 2018 report by the Institute of Policy Studies demonstrates that, even today, the African American unemployment rate is at least twice the White unemployment rate in 14 states.

5. The Median Wealth Aspect

It is an indisputable fact that systemic discrimination used in policy tools creates, maintains and even increases the racial wealth gap. Education opportunities, high-income-earning jobs in tech and full-time employment will start the process of building wealth for the millennials, but it cannot work the miracle of closing the wide gap that exists today.

Time for CHANGE

It is highly necessary to introduce major, targeted and sustained policy interventions to lessen and eventually bridge this gap. Things can be set back on track only by eliminating the injustice inflicted on people of color and starting a clean slate of equality. But it's even more important that people of color build focus on financial literacy and education and aggressively focus on the path of wealth building.

Let's get this money, y'all.

Chapter 10 - Steps that Modern Day Black Americans Can Take to Bridge the Racial Wealth Gap

"Go to work! Go to work in the morn of a new creation … until you have … reached the height of self-progress, and from that pinnacle bestow upon the world a civilization of your own." – Marcus Garvey

Black Americans have achieved incredible success in fields such as politics, tech, business, entrepreneurship, music, and film. Working diligently toward success, many of us have also managed to build considerable wealth. Just recently, American businessman and investor, Robert F. Smith paid off the Morehouse graduating class' debt.

Freeing 396 Morehouse graduates from student loan debt opens up countless opportunities. It's from this ONE gesture, that many graduates will create generational wealth for their families.

The wealth gap is still here, but we can focus our efforts on financial literacy and WEALTH.

When you start to view various aspects of this serious issue and delve a little deeper, it's easy to realize that this gap isn't going to vanish anytime soon.

The Wealth Gap Still Exists

While it is good news for marketers that the spending power of Black Americans is estimated to reach 1.54 trillion in 2022 from the current $ 1.3 trillion, this doesn't tell the real story.

Spending power refers to consumption and not to the existence of wealth.

Federal data indicates that Black American households held a low median of $11,000 of wealth in 2013.

Are we likely to amass more wealth in the coming years?

The shocking answer to this question is—Yes.

We MUST.

Foundation for Opportunities

Ensuring financial security for future generations is based on passing on generational wealth and financial assets to the next generation to utilize, add to, and build upon. It helps create a solid foundation to help them seize new opportunities, acquire higher education and better jobs, and maintain a better standard of living.

The roots of the racial gap are entrenched deeply in American history. Institutionalized racism and the accompanying bias and discrimination have marginalized Blacks in the country. Restricted access to information and opportunities as well as the selective distribution of American prosperity created enormous hurdles in the advancement of Black people.

However, there is a ray of hope. Look at what Rodney Sampson, the co-founder of Opportunity Hub (OHUB), the largest Black-owned multi-campus entrepreneurship center and technology hub in the U.S., has to say: "Black Americans through exposure, knowledge, and access to work, entrepreneurship, and investment opportunities in the innovation economy have the greatest opportunity to create new multi-generational wealth with no reliance on pre-existing multi-generational wealth."

The Time to Change Is Now

Let's see what modern-day Black Americans can do to create an atmosphere that will be conducive to wealth building.

"I built a conglomerate and emerged the richest Black man in the world in 2008 but it didn't happen overnight. It took me 30 years to get to where I am today. Youths of today aspire to be like me but they want to achieve it overnight. It's not going to work. To build a successful business, you must start small and dream big. In the journey of entrepreneurship, tenacity of purpose is supreme." – Aliko Dangote

1. Black Millennials Wield Enormous Power

In the new construct of Black wealth building, Black millennials have a crucial role to play in creating a financial legacy and reducing the Black-White wealth gap in the country. We have the advantage of education and innovative approach to better our chances of success.

Black millennials are more educated, dynamic, innovative and experimental than our ancestors. These qualities allow us to up the ante when it comes to creating and building wealth, which is something our forefathers were unable to achieve.

Millennials are set to be the largest generation and the most extensive section of the modern-day workforce. This also means Black millennials have the opportunity to grab a bigger slice of the pie and create wealth for future generations. This can go a long way in closing the wealth gap that exists today.

2. Focus on Building Credit

Generating wealth with the right opportunities and hard work is possible. However, building wealth is closely linked to saving money and creating credit.

Good credit improves economic status, and consistent savings help in the planning of buying assets. As we acquire wealth, understanding that credit is key will positively influence our approach to improving our economic status.

Having poor/no credit catalyzes the cycle of economic depression, which is prevalent in the American Black community, which hurts the efforts to build wealth. Although it isn't always easy to have discussions about credit with our loved ones, it's important to discuss these aspects. The idea is to focus on building credit as one of the cornerstones of wealth building.

3. Investment in Real Estate

For generations, people of color have been denied the opportunity to invest tangibly in real estate. Through the centuries, Blacks have had to face onerous lending terms or even outright refusal to lend, due to poor or lack of credit scores.

Investment in real estate is central to a plan of building generational wealth. As soon as you have some savings set aside, it's vital to shore up efforts to purchase a home in urban areas of the city you live in. It won't be long before a shift takes place in urban communities. The property values will slowly rise, making these areas desirable to live as well as invest in.

It's important for Black Americans to be vigilant and focused on planning our economic ascent. We can do this by investing in multi-unit housing and taking advantage of loans via first-time homebuyer programs.

There are a TON of resources available for those looking to utilize closing cost assistance, reduced interest rates and significantly lower down payment costs. You can browse programs by state by visiting this page: bit.ly/fthbprogram.

These can prove to be solid-income generating options, which in turn will bolster wealth.

According to the Economic Policy Group, "Housing equity makes up about two-thirds of all wealth for the typical (median) household."

It means that the wealth gap is typically a housing wealth gap. There is a long history of housing policies that were anti-Black. Acquiring loans, gaining access to specific neighborhoods and owning land were all nothing but a dream for Black Americans and redlining created a monumental challenge when it came to home ownership.

So, are Black millennials ready to enter the housing market?

With insufficient income in hand, 30% prefer to stay with their parents while 60% seek rental accommodation, says Goldman Sachs.

There needs to be a concerted effort to change our attitudes towards investing in real estate. Prudent investing in real estate is the first step on the path to building generational wealth.

The focus should be on moving out of a rental apartment and investing in cities that are in the formation stages. These places may not seem so attractive at the moment, but an increasing number of city residents are migrating to them.

The steadily increasing populations in these growing cities are matched by an increase in corporate set-ups there too. This means there are scores of upcoming multi-family properties in various sections in America that are available for purchase.

If Black millennials can focus on investing in real estate in these areas, we can rent them out and create cash flow. The income that flows in from these properties will give them the luxury of living rent-free if that's what they want. This is because the amount of money that flows into their pocket from renting out these properties will give them the money they need to pay their rent, all the while building an asset.

One quick-fire way to build your real estate portfolio is with a strategy called "House Hacking." Coined by the amazing folks at **BiggerPockets.com**, a real estate blog for investors, it's an option ANY first time home buyer can benefit from.

According to Bigger Pockets: "It is the real estate investing strategy   whereby you purchase a property for a low percentage down, live in one part of the property, and rent out the other parts such that the rent from your tenants (or roommates) exceeds your expenses. By doing this, you have likely significantly reduced or completely eliminated your living expense."

It's like buying a home and living rent free while someone ELSE pays off your mortgage!

Credit and student loan debt can become hurdles for millennials looking to invest in real estate. However, if you can increase your credit score to 580, there are federally-funded programs like the FHA mortgage program that can get you started. You'd only need to make a down payment of 3.5% towards your first home purchase. As per the rules of this program, buyers are required to live in that home for a minimum of 12 months. You could live in the home, rent out the additional rooms and live rent-free. PLUS, you would have an appreciating asset for decades to come.

4. HSA Has Some Distinct Advantages

Choosing the right investment account is an essential building block in wealth building. This implies opting for tax-favored accounts to strengthen your nest egg. For example, the Health Saving Account (HSA) is a powerful wealth-building instrument.

An HSA is a tax-advantaged medical savings account available to any and all taxpayers in the U.S. enrolled in a high-deductible health plan (HDHP). The funds contributed to this account are not subject to federal income tax at the time of deposit.

It is a relatively new introduction, and Congress established this in 2003. It offers many advantages.

HSA contributions are tax-deductible.

The withdrawals and investment gains are tax-free, too, when used to pay for specific medical expenses.

Millennials are the first generation to benefit from an HSA. Savings in these accounts can give us an early start in life, and we can invest without the burden of being taxed. If Black millennials plan to start the process of wealth building in their 30s, we cannot overlook this triple benefit that HSAs offer them.

You can start a Health Savings Account with your banks, financial advisor, credit union or insurance company.

5. Creating Wealth through the Stock Market

Most people consider investing in the stock market to be a risky proposition. The common understanding is that investing money, time and energy in something intangible is difficult. However, if your family considers wealth building a priority, it's vital to consider the stock market as an investment avenue.

African American participation is very dismal in the stock market.

As per a 2014 study by Credit Suisse and Brandeis University's Institute, the top 5% of African Americans invest a greater proportion of their wealth in lower-volatility assets relative to a White comparison group, including insurance, savings bonds and CDs. It also shows proportionally higher investments in real estate and proportionally lower investments in business assets.[17]

A market research report conducted in 2017 stated that approximately 67% of Black Americans with incomes of $50,000 and above had invested money in mutual funds or stocks. These figures were an improvement from 60% in 2010 and 57% in 1998.

Conducting research on the stock market and selecting stocks judiciously to invest in is a proven way of creating wealth in the long run.

Black Americans need to start looking at this option in earnest. You do not need piles of money to start investing in the stock market. You can start by investing small surpluses from time to time. The volatility of the stock market and the impact of business cycles make stock market investments seem like a risky proposition. However, this avenue carries substantial rewards as well, and you can expect a multifold appreciation of your investment in the long run.

If you are unsure about your understanding of the stock market and how to go about investing in it, you should consider joining an investment club.

Alternatively, you can engage the services of a certified financial planner as well. While you are researching various aspects of stock market investing, it's a good idea to consider investing in exchange-traded funds and mutual funds in a brokerage account.

Most employer-based retirement accounts make use of these investment instruments to dilute the risk of owning just a few stocks. There are many advantages to owning individual investment accounts in tandem with your retirement account such as:

- The income tax rates on your capital gains are generally lower than the income tax that you pay on tax-deferred withdrawals from your employer-sponsored retirement account.
- The withdrawals aren't subject to a penalty on an early withdrawal.
- In case you suffer any losses on the sale of stocks that can offset your income (based on IRS rules).

6. Entrepreneurship Is a Sure-Shot Way of Building Wealth

We live in an age when side hustles are almost the norm. Millennials are jumping onto the entrepreneurship bandwagon at a very rapid pace, and this is one of the fastest routes to wealth building. The future of work is firmly entrenched in the innovation economy. This concept focuses on studying which jobs will or may exist and the ones that might not in the future.

If Black Americans focus on working along the lines of the innovation economy and make inroads into the high-tech industries (which are largely knowledge-based), we will be in a better position to disrupt the disparities in wealth; while there may be certain advantages to working for big brands and global corporations, the upside can be very negligible in these companies.

It's time to shift our focus and look for work opportunities in startups that have good fund backing. Millennials would be in a better position to negotiate cash deals and also specific equity deals in these high-growth businesses.

This strategy will give millennials a good base and the funds needed to start their business ventures. Many enterprising Black millennials are seeking mentors and other resources like incubators to provide them with the boost they need to set off on the right foot to building wealth.

However, it's essential to be well-grounded and realize that a change will not happen overnight. We still need to be steady when it comes to saving and investing and understanding why the wealth gap exists. This can help us map a substantial legacy that will slowly tilt the scale in the favor of Black American families.

A Shift That Can Happen from Building Collective Economies

The need of the hour is to defocus from all the things that hindered in our progress. It's time to make a determined shift in our mindset and focus only on wealth building through collective economies. While buying properties is a major component of building a collective economy, it's equally important to invest in our communities.

We have discussed in detail that, for a large part of our nation's history, the policies that existed ensured that people of color would not be able to acquire loans, buy homes or even move into suburban areas. The equity that individuals have in their homes continues to be one of the most glaring differences between White and Black wealth.

But we have the resilience to beat these odds, stand tall and fight for our rights. Moreover, we also now live in a world where the field, if not level, has fewer potholes for Blacks than before.

Millennials now have the tools to start building wealth. Just as it's said that it's never too late to start, we'd also like to say that's it's never too early to start.

Do not put off saving or investing.

Start today because economic development is the cornerstone of a stable and successful community.

It's heartening to see that Black millennials are slowly but surely stepping up their wealth-building game. We are making a concerted and determined effort to develop financial plans and are attending seminars. We are asking questions and seeking answers that will set us on the path to wealth creation to give us the financial security we need.

More importantly, this will take us one step closer to bridging the racial wealth gap and changing the story of our people. We need to be determined and work hard towards building an ecosystem that will have a solid foundation of wealth and which will benefit the generations to come. More power to us!!

Credits

1. Whites Have Huge Wealth Edge Over Blacks (but Don't Know It)
    https://www.nytimes.com/interactive/2017/09/18/upshot/Black-White-wealth-gap-perceptions.html
2. Survey of Consumer Finances
    https://www.federalreserve.gov/econres/scfindex.htm
3. Survey of Consumer Finances
    https://www.federalreserve.gov/econres/scfindex.htm
4. Roberta Spalter-Roth and Terri Ann Lowenthal, "Race, Ethnicity, and the American Labor Market: What's at Work?" (Washington: American Sociological Association, 2005), available at
    http://www.asanet.org/sites/default/files/savvy/images/research/docs/pdf/RaceEthnicity_LaborMarket.pdf
5. How to Fight Back Against Mortgage Discrimination -
    https://www.wisebread.com/how-to-fight-back-against-mortgage-discrimination
6. The Ever-Growing Gap -
    https://ips-dc.org/wp-content/uploads/2016/08/The-Ever-Growing-Gap-CFED_IPS-Final-1.pdf
7. Cheer Up, America: 1,700 Millionaires Are Minted Every Day -
    https://www.bloomberg.com/news/articles/2016-11-21/cheer-up-america-1-700-millionaires-are-minted-every-day
8. How Much Home Can You Afford? Mortgage Rule of Thumb -
    https://www.thebalance.com/how-much-home-can-you-afford-mortgage-rule-of-thumb-1289846
9. An Introduction to 529 Plans -
    https://www.sec.gov/reportspubs/investor-publications/investorpubsintro529htm.html

10. How Teens are Spending Money - https://www.marketingcharts.com/demographics-and-au diences-80708

11. The Ultimate Guide to ETFs - https://money.usnews.com/investing/funds/articles/wh at-is-an-etf-the-ultimate-guide

12. Here's how much money you should have saved by 50 - https://www.cnbc.com/2018/10/19/how-much-money-you-should-have-saved-by-50.html

13. The Racial Wealth Gap: Addressing America's Most Pressing Epidemic - https://www.forbes.com/sites/brianthompson1/2018/0 2/18/the-racial-wealth-gap-addressing-americas-most-pre ssing-epidemic

14. White families have nearly 10 times...https://www.epi.org/blog/the-racial-wealth-gap-h ow-African Americans-have-been-shortchanged-out-of-the-materials-t o-build-wealth/

15. African Americans' Wealth A Fraction That Of Whites Due To Systematic Inequality - https://www.forbes.com/sites/christianweller/2019/02/ 14/African Americans-wealth-a-fraction-that-of-Whites-due-to-syste matic-inequality/#6b4ae4114554

16. Housing and Housing Finance - https://www.urban.org/urban-wire/what-explains-home ownership-gap-between-Black-and-White-young-adults

17. Credit Suisse Press Release - https://www.credit-suisse.com/corporate/en/articles/me dia-releases/42428-201411.html

ABOUT THE AUTHOR

John D. Saunders is an avid Financial Nerd, Digital Marketing Consultant and Entrepreneur.

As a student of financial literacy with the goal of generational wealth, John launched a small blog called **blackwallet.org** to provide urban millennials with the necessary tools to make informed decisions about investing and money.

Reaching over 500,000+ online users a month across multiple platforms, John's goal of "financial freedom for all" is possible by assisting his audience with the tools to make informed decisions about their finances.

John runs a Digital Marketing consulting agency with Fortune 500 clients focused on website development, marketing strategy and lead acquisition.

While searching for financial literacy resources for the urban community and not finding content geared toward people of color, John decided to leverage the power of his marketing agency online to launch **blackwallet.org**.

When he's not geeked out on creating generational wealth, John enjoys reading an awesome book and traveling the globe with his wife and son.

To contact John about media appearances, consulting or speaking at your next event, visit **JohnDSaunders.co**

To connect with John on Twitter and Instagram, search **@JohnDSaunders.**

To join his FREE, Facebook group discussing financial literacy, investing tips and empowerment, visit: facebook.com/groups/financialliteracytips.

43366214R00078

Made in the USA
San Bernardino, CA
14 July 2019